Nurturing Your Feminine Energy:

& The Rise of Divine Femininity

By Reemus

COPYRIGHT

Copyright © 2023 by Rahiem Bailey
All rights reserved.
Imprint: Booksmango Inc.
Name: Rahiem Bailey
Please direct all enquiries to the author.

This book or any portion thereof may not be reproduced or used in any manner whatsoever without the express written permission of the publisher, except for the use of brief quotations in a book review.
London, United Kingdom

For licensing enquiries, email:
ReemusBailey@GMAIL.com

This is the second part of the Femininity Series.

Volume 1: *Healing the Feminine Energy & The Wounds of Your Inner Child*

Volume 2: *Nurturing Your Feminine Energy & The Rise of Divine Femininity*

TABLE OF CONTENTS

INTRO 1
NURTURING 9
CREATIVITY 25
INTUITION 37
BEAUTIFY REALITY 61
SISTERHOOD 67
CONCLUSION 91

INTRO

The Character of The Empowered Feminine

- Loving nature
- Aware of her energetic state
- In tune with the energy around her
- Radiant vibe
- Appreciates sensitivity
- Creative
- Charming
- Carries herself with grace
- Gentle nature
- Quiet strength (subtle influence)
- Adaptable character
- Positive-minded
- Loves her softness
- Takes pride in receiving

All of us here on Earth are an expression of the oneness that is nature. We are all an extension of the divine source. So we are all connected in some way or another. When we heal each other, we heal the world. And when we heal the world, we heal ourselves.

A part of gaining contentment in life is the understanding of our nature, both on a spiritual and physical level. It determines our experience in the world and influences our behaviours.

One of the most influential aspects of our behaviour is the temperament of the energy that we project. So you would be smart to control your energetic state if you wish to be content.

In the case of the genders, this can include learning about one of the most dominating aspects of our lives: the expression of two spiritual energies which we have labelled the "masculine" and "feminine" energies. There is a reason that we label it according to gender, even though all of us have both energies in us.

It is because men *generally* exhibit behaviours that align with the characteristics of masculine energy. It is vice versa for women with feminine energy. When we consciously follow this pattern, it usually leads to internal peace.

Unfortunately, because of societal manipulation, it is difficult for many people to align with the energy that fulfils them. For example, many women think about feminine energy and assume that it's not suited to them. This reality is unfortunate, but it isn't hard to understand why.

In the Western world, we grow up in a culture that is greatly disconnected from nature. It's important to remember that we are just the mirroring expressions of the world we've grown up in.

Women have been disconnected from their feminine essence for many reasons and this disconnection has been encouraged consciously and subconsciously. The way we think, walk and talk expresses the energy or frequency we operate on. But whether it be through indoctrination, environmental set-up or childhood experiences, women have been put into a state of overt expression of masculine energy.

They have been pressured into relying on qualities attributed to the Masculine. While we all have access to both energies within us and both need to be expressed, we all have an essence that we *prefer* to express. We will feel content when our behaviours are predominantly aligned with either masculine energy or feminine energy.

Women feel a sense of confidence when their thoughts and movements align with feminine energy. Any natural preference to express something can only point to one conclusion: that the desire is indeed natural. We need to highlight this because some women think that femininity is not suited to them. But this is generally not true.

As a woman, you are the human expression of the feminine spirit. This is why you feel fulfilled when you tap into this energy. Femininity is for you because you are the embodiment of feminine energy itself. Never tell yourself otherwise.

In this book, not only are we going to go deeper into understanding the beautiful gift known as feminine energy, but also how to increase its expression. The goal is to increase your self-esteem and sense of self-empowerment. Much pleasure awaits along this journey.

Femininity Is About Energy

One of the most important things to consider is that feminine energy is exactly that: energy. It's not a specific thing or even a specific action. Feminine energy doesn't automatically mean "pink dresses" or that you *have* to do your hair in a certain way. No.

Of course, certain things can make you feel feminine and it's what we will discuss in this book. But the most critical part is how you *feel* from within. If you do all the external actions but do not *feel* feminine then the actions are worthless.

If you've done the work to *Heal the Feminine Energy: & The Wounds of Your Inner Child*, then this will come more naturally. Healing work opens the space that allows feminine behaviour to have an effect.

All actions suggested in this book, or by any other educational resource, are simply to achieve the goal of helping you to *feel* feminine. You are free to adjust the suggestions that you read according to what achieves this goal.

NURTURING

The Blessing of Nurturing

Nurturing is a vital element of femininity. The power to nurture is one of the superpowers that are exclusive to women. But first, let's get into the definition of this quality:

"To nurture"

- *To take care of, feed and protect someone or something, to help him, her or that thing to develop.*
- *To help a plan or person develop and be successful.*
- *To nourish, encourage and care for someone or something.*

When we read the definition of the word, is there anything about it that should be looked down on? Doesn't it sound like something that should be greatly appreciated? Can you see how these qualities are necessary to both men and women, as well as children and communities?

Nurturing is necessary for the growth of an individual and even fostering a positive spiritual or mental state. This is why femininity is a necessary part of human life.

Unfortunately, current society does not give 'nurturing' the credit it deserves. Many people limit their admiration of a woman's nurturing powers by only admiring their ability to give birth. However, this superpower extends to more than just that.

But before this power can be given to anyone else, it's important to give it to yourself. You deserve to benefit from the beauty of your own nurturing first. This is what enables you to share it with a world that needs it.

Nurture Yourself

You will see the true power of nurturing after you begin to benefit from it. This will include going on an expedition to nurture your strengths, skills and characteristics. Going on a journey of self-development is the key to increasing divine femininity.

You must begin to get excited about being on a path of growth. Give yourself the chance to look back in a year or two and say to yourself: "Wow. Look how far I've come and what I've become".

The areas which you must develop are:

- Physical health and fitness.

- Spiritual health and energetic frequency.

- Mental health and emotional state.

Do not set the bar low. You are not just trying to be someone who is getting by in life and surviving. The goal is to thrive as the most empowered version of yourself. Why would you want anything less?

Go as deep as possible and see this work as just as important as you would view your job. The rewards will be worth it as you begin to view yourself as the highest expression of divinity. You will start becoming the type of person that you dream of being.

Doing "shadow" work means developing different aspects of yourself. You are working on living the life that you deserve. Getting to this level requires working on areas of improvement that might be uncomfortable.

You have to identify emotional triggers and areas of your life where you lack faith. But do not be harsh on yourself. Simply see these as obstacles that are keeping you from your higher self. This is all a part of nurturing yourself.

If you can, seek out other people who can guide you along this path of self-mastery.

Mentorship is an extremely important thing. You could even consider going to therapy. And depending on what type of person you are, seek out religious, spiritual or life coaches.

However, you do not have to rely on anyone else to begin making self-growth a daily habit. You can start by structuring your life so that you are progressing every day. It's important to start the day how you would want to see it through.

One good rule to live by is to never go a day without doing something that nurtures your mind, body or spirit. Even when you're taking rest breaks, this still counts as growth because it is all a part of the process of self-development.

Having alone time is important, and not just for self-care activities but for introspection and reflecting on where you are. Often, we get so tangled in a situation that we forget to look at ourselves from an outside perspective.

When you are alone, this is the time to meditate or pray. It is the time to connect to yourself, understanding what your needs and goals are. Embracing alone time gives you the space to plan and regain your thoughts.

Stop to reflect on the things in life that are working for you and the things that aren't. This helps you to adjust the strategy of self-work so that you can become better at nurturing yourself. You'll gain a lot of self-esteem when you see the seeds that you planted in yourself.

Think of these plants as being the flowers that represent your internal value. And like you would nurture any plant in the external world, you are watering the most important ones of all: the ones that are within you.

EXERCISE: NO PEOPLE-PLEASING

One problem that a feminine woman might have is that she nurtures others even when she's feeling depleted. But it's crucial to fill your cup before you fill others. Your 'cup' is your source of energy. You must be selective with it, only allowing it to flow into sources that replenish you.

So understand the power of the words "yes" and "no." One of the most empowering things you can do is to get out of the habit of saying "yes" to things that do not feel aligned. Practice saying "no" when you don't have the energy to accommodate certain requests.

You come first and you should not be ashamed to embrace this. This puts you in a position to nurture others. Only say "yes" when it is authentic. Stop saying yes when you do not feel the feeling of "yes" inside.

Be aware of your emotional and energetic state after you engage in different activities. In your journal, make a note of the activities that bring your vibe down. Then record the events that raise your vibrations.

Drop the tasks that ruin your vibe. If some of them are necessary, find out how you can make them more enjoyable. If this can't be done, then see if the activity can be delegated.

Nurture Others

Once you've done the work to nurture yourself, you are now in a position to nurture others. Women who have worked on themselves are of more value to their partners, family and community. Plus, nurturing others is one way to stimulate your feminine state.

It's important to care for something other than yourself. This could be done in many ways, such as caring for something or encouraging the development of someone else. The main point is to indulge in the feeling of pure love that comes from selfless service as you bring pleasure to others.

In a culture that promotes ruthless competition and selfish independence, it is an act of rebellion to take pride in being of service to others. These are the principles that help to foster an environment that is benevolent and loving.

Selfless acts of nurturing could be: baking a cake for your partner or knitting a hat for your niece. Enjoy seeing the joy on their faces when they receive it. Another example includes surprising your friend with a day out just to remind her to take a break. Alternatively, it could just be showing someone that you are *fully* attentive as they speak to you about what they are going through.

Do not do these things to tick a box off the list. Truly feel the pleasure that comes from bringing positivity to other people and the appreciation that they give you in return. This all reinforces in your mind that you are an expression of value.

If the people who surround you are not worthy to receive your blessings, then you are not around the right people. There may be worries that this goodness will be taken for granted.

But this is why an empowered feminine woman needs to be selective.

Don't be the "people pleaser." Only give goodness to the people who deserve to receive it. When you share your energy, it should only go to people who return the same energy back to you. If your energy is going towards people that are not replenishing you in return, then stop. Reciprocation of value is needed in order to replenish your spirit.

Nurturing is also not limited to other people, but it's also for other living things. This could mean plants or animals. They cannot consciously reciprocate like humans can, but their innocent presence is enough to make you feel good.

Consider getting a plant in your living room or growing fruits in your garden. Don't just water it every day for the sake of it. Truly enjoy the process of caring for another living thing and watching it grow. This is all in the spirit of a nurturer.

Motherhood

One of the powers of feminine energy is that it aids the growth of the things it comes into contact with. This is why women are naturally better nurturers than men. In many ways, we already understand this, as proven by the fact we describe nature as "Mother Nature."

Just like how nature harnesses the power of the feminine energy to take seeds and bring forth plants, so too does a woman take the Masculine's seed to birth a baby.

Childbirth is arguably the most significant act of nurturing that a woman can do. It is no small deal that women can take a duo of cells and nurture it into four, eight, sixteen and so on until it is an entire being that consists of trillions of cells.

We often forget how miraculous this ability is because it is such a common occurrence. But remembering and revering the valuable powers of the Feminine is important because it helps us to maintain a high respect for femininity.

Not only is a woman necessary for birthing a baby, but the care she gives is necessary for producing a healthy adult. This is not something to be taken lightly. And if you are a mother, then you should seize the opportunity to be fully present as you nurture your child.

The way you nurture a child is a good reflection of how you nurture yourself and the others that are around you.

As we said earlier, the *first* person you must nurture is *you*. Many of the qualities that we will go through are things that you should be giving to yourself.

So even if you don't have a child, just apply the same concepts to the inner child that is within you. You deserve the same type of care that inspires the highest level of internal security and satisfaction.

Nurturing Your Child

Parents are expected to provide nutrition, shelter and clothing. However, there are also other things that you provide your child with that help to mentally nurture them to adulthood.

Shift your awareness to the pure love that you feel when you are creating a positive atmosphere for your child. This is what supports their development in the best possible way. Doing so will give you the pleasure that comes from being a nurturer and there is no other situation where you can do this more than with your child.

Presence: When you are interacting with your child, be as present as possible. It may even require you to turn off the phone so that you can be properly attentive. It is also a good opportunity to practise the power of listening.

Listen to your child verbally and non-verbally. Read their cues. It also helps to research the developmental stages of children so that you can be fully aware of where they are at, helping you to aid their growth.

Encouragement: One of the greatest traits of a good nurturer is that they are incredibly encouraging to their child and they do not get into a habit of discouraging. This requires having qualities like patience, effective communication and empathy. Teach your child that fear is normal and negative feelings like frustration are a natural part of life. It's important to let them know that they have the power to channel these emotions in a healthy manner.

Practise the art of positive talk and *never* tell them things that are discouraging. Instead, help them understand the difficulty of certain goals they have but let them know that if anyone can do it, they can! Be loud and proud about their talents. Be in awe of how gifted they are and be heavily invested in their interests.

Safety: We all need to feel secure. This is especially the case for children of all ages. Nothing can be truly nurtured in environments where safety is not assured. It's one of the reasons why women become more in tune with their feminine energy when they are with masculine men who make them feel safe.

In the case of your child, they should know for an absolute fact that their parents have their back. In the same way that a lion cub will run behind a lioness when it feels frightened, your child should seek you for protection.

You must keep them away from environments and people who are negative. This mindset also helps you to set a standard when choosing men to date or have children with (because you will vet them based on these principles).

Role model: Keep in mind that you are not just raising a human to physical maturity, but you are also setting the context that they are going to emotionally operate from for the rest of their life.

Many adults that we'd label as toxic are usually victims of their toxic upbringing. They were not given the type of nurturing that they needed. When you see a person treating their partner badly, it is likely that they did not grow up in a nurturing, loving environment. So they are simply mimicking the relationships that they've grown up around.

Homes that lack an abundance of nurturing are also responsible for many women allowing their partners to treat them horrendously. They may not have seen their mothers receive genuine treatment, so they may not have learned what healthy love looks like.

Though you may never be perfect, just keep in mind that *everything* that you see shapes the future much more than you know.

CREATIVITY

Be creative

As we discussed in the first volume, women who excessively express masculine energy end up creating a life based on the hardness that they've become attached to. Their daily activities reflect the protective masculine shell which they have created out of trauma.

The opposite of that scenario is the woman whose habitual practices align with the softness of femininity. So it's important to cultivate a lifestyle that supports your creativity and sense of freedom. The same gifts that make women able to nurture life are the same ones that make them creative beings.

A feminine woman lives with adventurousness in mind. She doesn't live restricted by the rigidity that modern culture encourages. Like a painter would treat a blank canvas, she treats her life in the same way.

Her life is her art. She is the paintbrush, her experiences are the paint and she seeks to create a masterpiece that has all the vibrancy, detail and abstract beauty she could ever ask for. The Feminine is in touch with her imagination and being creative is one way to tap into this quality.

When you feel fearful about living with such freedom, it is a result of you living in your head. You are overthinking with fear of failure and judgement. But as you continue to develop yourself, these issues will disappear and life will truly become your canvas.

All energy desires to be expressed and this is certainly the case when it comes to the creative energy of the Feminine. You need an outlet that allows this energy to play. This helps you to feel alive, rather than someone who is just existing and going through the monotonous routine of life.

Set time aside for hobbies that bring you pure enjoyment and release. And what you'll find is that certain activities give you a therapeutic effect. Ask yourself: what are the talents you have or the hobbies that bring you joy?

If you haven't given much time to your hobbies recently, think back to when you were a kid. What did you enjoy doing? What were you good at? If you did not get the chance to participate in these things when you were a kid, then it's time to now find a new hobby. It's never too late!

It doesn't need to be something that you're perfect at. That defeats the purpose of doing it in the first place. It's supposed to be the thing you do that allows you to let go and fully enter your body. Do not worry about the destination or even the result. Simply immerse yourself in the experience and do not worry about anything else.

Creative self-expression:

Creativity can either be expressed through art or technology.

Examples include:

- Photography (either taking photos or modelling)
- Content creation (vlogging and social media)
- Attending acting classes
- Drawing
- Colouring
- Painting
- Gardening
- Writing (fiction or nonfiction)
- Cooking
- Sewing/knitting
- Making new strategies for your business (from a place of creativity)
- Playing instruments
- Performing arts: Singing, acting, dancing

Some things on the list may not seem like they are related to creativity, but I would invite you to investigate things from a different perspective. Let's take cooking as an example. Food is a splendid example of something that is made from a place of nurturing.

When you are making a meal, you are making your unique version of the recipe. The finishing piece is created from your creative decisions and your unique touch. This is why the same ingredients can result in extraordinarily different tastes according to who made the dish. There are so many things that can be a creative project for you to pour into.

If you want to do something creative as a professional pursuit then the finished product is something that you will naturally care about. But that is okay too, as long as you stay true to your authenticity.

Many people want to share their creative pursuits with the world, but they fear others judging them. You might fear chasing your dream of being a music artist because of how your family will view you. Perhaps you want to be a content creator that makes educational videos about cooking but you are scared of unsupportive friends ridiculing you.

No matter what it is, don't let fear of how others may view you stop you. Be committed to doing what aligns with your heart. It's easy to hold it in so that you remain inconspicuous. But this is why authentic expression is an act of bravery that your feminine spirit will be thankful for. This level of vulnerability is something that allows your feminine energy to flourish.

Fortunately, your inner child is not the only person that will be thankful for your courage. So will the rest of the world. Your creative passions serve a purpose that bring value to others. For example, if you're a fashion designer, your designs are not just nice pieces of material. For someone else, they are more than that. They allow that person to feel proud about who they are. They are expressions of their character.

If you are a musician, your music is not just a collection of sounds. To some people, your music is the cure for their depression or the thing that helps them feel that they are understood. If you are a photographer, your pictures are not just images on a screen. To someone out there, they are reminders of how beautiful the world is and why they should always be grateful.

The creative talents that we were divinely blessed with bring value to others. The reward for you is that you receive the satisfaction of feeling your feminine energy stimulated.

Career

Creative expression alleviates the monotony of corporate culture. People are encouraged to give up on their passions to soullessly pursue money. Creative hobbies are especially good if you live with a strict routine that is not pleasurable. Doing a job that you hate is damaging to your feminine energy.

The empowered woman treats her life like art and goes through life drawing pleasure out of her daily experiences. She is deeply in tune with her internal state. When she enjoys what she is doing daily, it makes it easier for her to shift focus into her body.

Though it's also true that men shouldn't do a job that they hate, the concept of the Masculine doing this out of his duty to provide makes sense. This is not the same for the Feminine. Her most prized contribution is her nurturing ability, which cannot be shared if she feels depleted.

Men take pride in their exhaustive efforts. Women are the opposite. Working a job that does not align with your gifts and passions is a guaranteed way to be tired. The vibrancy of life drains away and your softness begins to disappear when you live like this.

It is not the career itself that you should value. It is the creative expression that speaks to your heart which you should see as your true "job." You were not made to work for money. You were made to be a valued member that offers service to your family, as well as your community.

Consider the type of career that resonates with you. Never prioritise money over fulfilment. What good is extra money if it makes you miserable? In the modern world, there are many ways to attract financial abundance while pursuing your talents and passions.

EXERCISE: FIND THE RIGHT JOB

Try to search for a new job or new position. Do not give up until you begin to attract what you deserve. Although it may be necessary sometimes to do jobs out of necessity, you want to create enjoyable sources of income.

Find a job that suits your personal qualities and preferences. When you don't enjoy your job, you are doing it out of survival or pure provision. This is not the empowered expression of femininity, it is a scarcity mindset. You do not need to settle.

Feminine Leisure

Even if you cannot do a job that supports your feminine energy, do leisurely activities that nurture that side of you. Take time out to do things for the sole purpose of enjoyment. Make this a priority in your life.

If possible, commit to making it frequent. Don't let the regularity of these activities make you feel like it's a chore. It's time well spent. When you engage in hobbies that are fulfilling, you are investing in your spiritual health.

The return on investment when you are doing pleasurable hobbies and relaxing activities is that it increases your feminine energy.

Since the feminine energy is flow, doing movement-based activities powerfully nourishes your spirit. This is a woman's way of being the physical expression of femininity. Moving the body encourages you to feel a sense of freedom and vitality. When you feel physically stuck, your energy is stifled.

The physical activities do not have to be extravagant. It could be as simple as starting your day with a ten-minute stretch in the morning or doing workouts that encourage you to work on your breathing and flexibility. Zumba and yoga sessions are activities that are also good for this.

Another activity that adds an aura of creativity is dance. Dancing is particularly reaffirming to your femininity. Own the movement of your body and be aware of how it feels to physically flow.

Music is stimulating too. It is the thing that drives the dancing itself. On weekends, when you find yourself doing domestic tasks, turn up the songs and let the music tease your senses. Then, when you feel the spontaneous urge to move, go where your spirit takes you.

The key is to focus on receiving the pleasure that comes with all these activities. This is the perfect time to leave your mind's worries and shift all focus to within. It's in the body where contentment eagerly awaits you.

INTUITION

One of the most prominent gifts of a spiritually in-tune being is the ability to connect to one's intuition. It's something that we all have access to. But this relies on a person's ability to tap into their internal state. So this makes it no surprise to hear that women have a deeper connection to this power.

Femininity is all about relating to the internal state. It explains why women are given credit for being masters of the spiritual realm. She's able to deeply connect to more than just the surface level and the material world. But to do this, she needs to heal the communication between her soul, body and mind.

Intuitive connection elevates her awareness to new heights. It makes being in your feminine state worth it. You benefit from receiving communication from higher levels of consciousness that transcend different areas of your life.

A Personal GPS

Your intuition is a trustable pilot that helps you to make decisions. It gives you a level of internal security that allows you to love life, with less reason to worry about where you are heading. You can trust in divine guidance.

Intuition is an inner knowing that is separate from conscious thought. It is instinctive and it comes from within. It can be accessed simply by "being." But you don't use it by sitting around and waiting for the knowledge to come to you. You must learn how to connect with it so that you can get the best out of it.

Your intuition is like an internal GPS that knows what is best for you. This GPS is programmed with wisdom that your conscious mind has not yet come across. So it is separate from the part of you that is always actively thinking.

Your mind processes all the "logic." All the mental chatter that you live through everyday occurs here. The mind is always processing words, numbers and technical pieces of information from the physical reality.

On the other hand, your intuition is a phenomenon of the subconscious mind. It is related to your spiritual body. Amazingly, it gives us the ability to understand something instinctively without the need to logically rationalise it. An intuitive woman will simply know what path to take without needing conscious reasoning.

What you will find is that whenever you go against your intuition, you will regret it. But whenever you listen to your subconscious messaging, you will always be grateful. This remains true even if you can't explain how you knew that it was the right decision.

As a woman, you are lucky to be so in tune with your intuition. Embrace this gift that adds another layer to the human experience. It's there to make your life better. Do not waste it.

Accessing Intuition

Your intuition can be thought of as being your "inner voice." It is constantly telling you things that help you to navigate the world. The inner voice can alert you of potential danger or advise you to heal certain areas that you need to work on. It's the subtle nudge you feel that puts you in the right direction.

If you want to access your internal GPS, the first step is to declare that you trust your intuition. Make the decision right now that you want to trust yourself and all the wisdom that lies within you. The information is there. But you will not be able to access it if you do not believe it.

You may be wondering: if intuition is such a natural part of us, then why do we have trouble connecting to it? It goes back to the detachment that this Western society has from nature. This is a problem because connecting to your intuition requires connecting to your internal state. This is hard to do in a world that is disconnected from nature.

Additionally, the modern world pushes us into our "head" rather than into our "body." Femininity is about connecting with the body. As we navigate this physical world, we are dependent on the use of the mind. The bombardment of content in the modern age can be extremely overwhelming.

Consequently, we don't get much practice listening to our inner voice so the noise of the outer world drowns it out. One of the main things that tune down the inner voice's volume is the value we place on the voices of other people.

No one teaches us how to trust our inner voice and how to nurture its communication with us. Instead, people are taught to ignore their intuition (in covert and overt ways).

Examples of this could include you feeling ashamed for trying to rely on intuition when making decisions. You may have 'just had a feeling' that something was not right about a particular situation. But since you were not able to rationalise it with a cohesive, logical explanation, other people did not take it seriously.

So unfortunately, people struggle to trust their voices and may only feel that their decisions are valid when other people approve of them. You end up replacing your inner voice with the guidance of others and it becomes an endless habit.

This is severely damaging to our self-confidence and the trust that we have in ourselves. It's difficult to trust yourself when you do not even value your decision-making. It's no surprise then that people do not give intuition the admiration that it deserves.

Listen to The Inner Voice

There's nothing wrong with making decisions based on pure practicality and logic. This is necessary for many situations. However, a world in which intuition is not valued takes away the connection to such a great gift. Intuition adds an extra dimension to our decision-making.

After pledging to trust your intuition, it's time to understand how to receive messages from this divine source. Your intuition doesn't communicate with you in the same technical manner as the mind. It will never come to you as a set of logical instructions handed to you as an easy-to-read guidebook. It doesn't work like that.

Though we may call intuition your "inner voice," it speaks non-verbally. Guidance comes via sensations. It is not the sensation itself that is the divine source, but the sensation is just one way it can get the message to you.

Think of it like someone sending a message to you. The message could be delivered as a letter, text message, word-of-mouth or a voice message. That is similar to our intuition.

It has multiple modes of communication that can make you aware of the message. These can include emotions, thoughts, feelings, dreams and even physical issues. Listen to and observe the sensations when they come.

The next step is then to interpret the sensations. This requires being a very good listener. You must be present and patient as the message flows to you. Over time, it will become natural to listen to your inner voice and you will be able to gain instant clarity as the message comes.

One of the reasons that intuition is a dependable guide is because it passes on data from different parts of you. This includes your electromagnetic field, but it also includes your heart. It is communicating all the information that your conscious mind is not processing. This is why you get certain subconscious feelings when you are in particular situations.

Your body is processing the information that it is receiving in the present moment. This is a part of the nature of the Feminine. She is very present. Knowing this matters because you may have planned to do or say specific things for the scenarios that you are in.

Your inner voice may have a different plan though. If you block out its messages in favour of the script you had in your mind, you will drown it out. Your inner voice is most likely going to talk to you while you're in the pressure of the moment. And even if you don't have a conscious plan, trusting your inner voice will ensure that you'll be okay.

When the sensation manifests as a thought or a 'knowing', this is confirmation that you have made sense of the inner voice. You should always listen to it. Trust it. This helps to assure you that no matter what situation you are in, you'll always be okay because your intuition will be there to guide you. The more you honour listening to yourself, the more it will serve you.

Converse With The Inner Voice

It is one thing to receive intuitive messages. It's another thing to go back and forth with the inner voice in a conversation.

Keep in mind that you'll not always be able to interpret the sensations you receive. It may not 'make sense' at first and you will have to sit with it until clarity comes. This can take time.

But there is one way to speed up the process. As the saying goes, if you don't understand something then don't be afraid to ask questions. Treat your inner voice like this. Ask yourself questions and have an internal conversation.

Some questions to ignite conversation:

- What are you trying to let me know?
- I'm here to listen. Can you show me the way?
- I trust you. What should I do?
- What are you?
- Why are you here? What are you trying to tell me?
- What is the truth that I am closing my eyes to?
- I know the answer is already here. What am I missing?

Then listen to the answers. They will be sensations of a subconscious nature. They may give a feeling of premonition, sudden realisation or contentment.

Many times, because of the present nature of the feminine energy, you will feel the answer instantly. It can also help to try to interpret the sensations with vibrant descriptions. For example, if the message was a colour, a sound, an image or an object, what would it be? This helps you to translate the internal feeling into something more tangible and easier to understand.

However, the reply can also take some time. That's okay too. Just trust that the replies will come when you need them. Just make sure you provide the space for the inner voice to speak. This helps quiet mental chaos as much as possible. After a while, you will begin to see the difference between your mental chatter and the messages from your heart.

Take Action

The next step is to act on your intuition. What good is the information that's being gifted to you if you do not decide to use it? The purpose of intuition is to guide you. So, after you receive the information and know which direction it is encouraging you to go in, proceed to take those steps.

It will take time to trust it, but your confidence will rise when your actions begin to birth a stream of positive results. This enthusiasm will begin to spread to other areas of your life too.

Perhaps you have been procrastinating on something that you know you need to do. Intuitive hits can encourage you to do the things that you know you should've started. It may be to start going to the gym, to write that book or to start that coaching business. Whatever it is, the inner voice wants the best for us and will tell you what needs to be worked on. If you ignore it, you will be forced to listen to it in other ways.

Neglecting your intuition may activate a sense of "dissatisfaction." It could manifest as depression or frustration. This discomfort is the intuitive voice whispering in your ear. But the more you ignore it, the more it will speak to you.

If you still do not listen, then your 'gut instinct' might communicate with you through your gut and other body parts. This can include disease and illnesses. Don't allow it to get to that point.

Working on your mental health helps to interpret the inner voice accurately. When you are operating on an unhealthy frequency, without self-love and mental stability, you will incorrectly translate the messages that you are receiving.

Cleanse your mind and heal your issues so that it doesn't distort mind-body communication. The more work you do, the more this interpretation of the intuition will become pure.

Don't put too much pressure on yourself when you begin listening to your inner voice. It will begin as a faint whisper and with consistency, it will become a familiar voice that you couldn't ignore if you tried. The more you listen, the more you receive. Over time, your feminine spirit will reward you with the answers you need, knowing that you trust it.

EXERCISE: SOCIAL MEDIA DETOX

Constantly consuming content makes it hard to connect to your voice. This is because your brain is always processing the voices of other people and not your own. It also puts all your awareness in your head. And you can't 'logic' your way into feminine energy. You need to connect to your body.

So it's good to take breaks from technology and simply sit with yourself. Mindful activities such as meditation and yoga help with this. Other activities include going for solo walks in nature, bike rides in the city or even doing self-care activities. And if you have the time, you could also go on countryside city breaks and wellness retreats.

Perhaps not surprisingly, intuitive whispers will often come when you are doing creative activities. When you are expressing creativity, you enter a state of flow and internal presence. This is where communication happens.

Connect to Nature

Since being in a world that is disconnected from nature can suffocate your femininity, then being in nature nourishes your femininity. The Earth's playground heavily mimics the qualities of the feminine spirit.

Mother Nature gives life, giving the space for the seeds of divinity's creations to blossom and bloom. She provides the nutrients needed for all life to sustain itself. She is sacred and the simple sight of her is awe-inspiring. She can be volatile and she promotes adventure. Mother Nature is also at her most functional when there is an abundance of collaboration.

There are so many benefits that come with connecting to nature. There's a reason we say "Mother Nature" when we speak about the Earth and all life that comes from her. Mother

Nature is one of the greatest examples of nurturing. Connecting to her is one way to nurture many aspects of yourself.

The physical construction of modern-day cities is aligned with the qualities of the masculine energy. This is not a surprise considering that it was the Masculine that constructed the modern world. From our buildings and the technology that we use, to the systems and routines we operate on, it has all come from the Masculine. The manifestation of our modern world is an expression of hardness. It is linear and static, which are qualities that are attributed to masculine energy.

The dull and monotonous vibe of our modern cities is much different from Mother Nature's expression. This is not necessarily a good or bad thing. But when you look at nature, there is more flow, curvature and vibrancy in the environment. Nature provides a palette of colours, possibilities and adventure. These are traits that are extremely stimulating to feminine energy.

When you go out into nature, it naturally brings you into your body. Your senses are stimulated, including the sights that affect your eyes and the scents that arouse your nose, the breeze that touches your skin and the sounds that tease your ears. Nature brings novelty to your day, providing freedom from the routine of daily life.

This is why travelling nurtures your feminine energy. But novelty is not limited to overseas experiences. There are so many local experiences that can tingle your senses. Take the mindset that you would have when you are travelling and apply it to the experiences you have in your country.

Activities in nature that stimulate the senses:

- Safari trips or farm visits.
- Long walks or jogs in the park or forest.
- Hiking.
- Wild swimming.

The goal is to be as present as possible. Make sure that you feel grounded as you detach from technology and all the worries that come with it. Vacations are not the only way to do this. You can do this by being in nature.

It is very likely that when you are one with Mother Nature, you will get many intuitive hits and messages. As we said, we can struggle to listen to the inner voice because of our detachment from nature. When you mend this relationship, you mend the connection you have within yourself.

Earthing and Grounding

Grounding is a therapeutic experience that helps you to make a connection to the Earth's core. Our bodies carry a positive electrical charge that builds up in our bodies. When we make contact with Mother Nature's surface, we tap into the Earth's negative charge that allows us to cleanse ourselves of any 'excess' energy.

This practice has a healing effect. It reduces depression and anxiety, reduces stress chemicals, decreases pain and speeds up our recovery time. It creates safety within your nervous system and it restores balance in your body.

Grounding can be done both outdoors and indoors. It depends on the technique that you want to use. 'Earthing' can be as simple as walking barefoot on natural ground for 20 minutes at a time. You can place your entire body on the grass, in the sand or in the sea.

When doing this practice indoors, you can sit on a specialised grounding mat. The benefit of this method is that it helps to ground you throughout the entire day.

While you sit down, imagine connecting to the core of the Earth. It may feel weird at first but it will eventually feel natural.

Crystals

They say that "diamonds are a girl's best friend." Therefore it's safe to assume that on some level, we are a species that strongly values crystals. But for our divinely connected ancestors, this went much further. They had much appreciation for the beauty of crystals and the powers that they hold.

Crystals are packets of crystallised frequencies that can be considered to be sentient beings. They emit frequencies just like living animals and plants do. Some people would even go as far as to say that crystals are not far from being considered alive.

Just like living animals, crystals have various species. Each species looks different and has properties that make them unique. But more importantly, they have different effects on us.

When they are charged and activated, their frequencies interact with our body's energy field.

Without the technology that we have today, our ancestors were able to realise that different crystals have certain effects on mental, physical and spiritual health. Some are known to have healing effects, while others can boost confidence.

Getting the benefits from crystals is pretty simple. Simply place your crystals on or near your body. And the crystal emits positive vibrations that interact with your body.

EXERCISE: GO CRYSTAL SHOPPING

Different crystals have different positive effects. But since we have been discussing intuition, we will look into the crystals that help empower your intuitive powers.

- **Moonstone** - Known for its healing effects, this stone is credited for enhancing intuition and stabilising emotions. It is especially powerful on full moons.

- **Moldavite** - It's an extra-terrestrial stone that comes from a meteor. It is a chakra opener and it works with your heart. Your heart is the chief commander when it comes to your intuition, so this is perfect if you want to connect to your inner voice.

- **Labradorite** - This crystal is very spiritually endowed. Labradorite protects your energetic atmosphere and helps you communicate to the higher vibrational version of yourself. It's said to help you connect with your past lives, helping you to receive divine guidance.

- **Apophyllite** - It is a lightly coloured crystal that helps to link the spiritual world with the physical one. It is believed to enhance our psychic abilities.

- **Amethyst** - This is a well-known stone that activates our spiritual wisdom and can even help us understand our dreams. It helps us to interpret the inner voice by calming the mind and fostering focus.

- **Lapis Lazuli** - It's a stone that connects us to the inner truth and increases our intelligence. It also helps soothe our nervous system, providing a calm internal environment that makes it easier to hear intuition's whisper.

- **Clear Quartz** - This stone encourages mental clarity and emotional stability. It inspires our focus, which is essential for understanding ourselves and new perspectives.

BEAUTIFY REALITY

It should be no surprise that the expression of beauty nurtures femininity. An empowered feminine woman has a very beautiful internal state and projects that externally. She radiates charm and appeal that manifests on a physical level.

Many women must tell themselves that it's okay to like girly things and expressions of prettiness. Heal your perception of beauty and your feminine spirit will be grateful. Depending on your experiences, you may have to unlearn your beliefs on these issues.

You may have to tell yourself that it is okay to like gentleness, cuteness, expressions of softness and anything else you can think of. These are all things that help you to feel more feminine.

Beautify Yourself

Before your feminine glow can affect others, you must first allow it to be projected onto yourself. One way to do this is to embrace the projection of your physical beauty. So connect to your facial and bodily beauty. Your presentation is an expression of your feminine frequency.

Many people put women down for putting effort into looking good. But as long as there is not a strong attachment to external validation, you should embrace being as beautiful as you want. Never feel ashamed for wanting to put extra effort into your appearance.

Just make sure that it is done for your own satisfaction, as opposed to being for other people. When you look good, you feel good. And when you feel good, you want to look good too. It is a positive cycle that helps to increase your self-confidence. But the cycle doesn't stop there.

People will treat you according to the standard that you set. Of course, the priority of your beauty is always for you. But its effect on others (which, in turn, is a reaffirmation of who you are) cannot be denied. This also includes beautifying your skin and getting on a daily skincare routine.

Invest time and energy into figuring out what materials make you feel feminine. And there are many areas in which you must be conscious of doing this. This includes your clothes, hair, makeup and more.

Dressing in a girly manner can make you feel feminine. But on the other hand, dressing in masculine clothes can make it harder to embrace feminine energy.

One of the other issues with manly clothing is that it represents the vibe that you're projecting to the world. You don't have to wear bright colours or dresses, but you should be cautious of the signal that you're putting out.

Beautify your body

Your feminine spirit is nurtured when your clothes exude beauty. But if clothes can have that effect, what impact do you think having a beautiful body could have? Care for your body and decide to get in the best shape that you can. This means cleaning your diet and sticking to your workout schedule.

Getting in great shape is an act of self-love. It is treating your body with the reverence that it deserves. It also gives you more reason to love every part of your body. You might be someone that already loves your body without it being in the best possible shape. But imagine how much *more* you would love it when it's in even better shape.

Your body will be another affirmation of your beauty. This is one of the biggest side effects of eating right and exercising. It's not just physically beneficial. It is very mentally empowering.

When you stick to a disciplined schedule and you see that you're able to excel at something, it gives your mind proof that you are powerful. Your morale will have no choice but to rise.

You don't have to push yourself too much. It's not about making huge strides to rush to a certain result. Remember, femininity is process oriented. The journey itself is what you must appreciate.

Start small and remain consistent. If buying one healthy snack a day is progress for you, that's good enough. If getting up in the morning and doing a three-minute workout is enough, then that's fine. For you, it could be taking the stairs instead of the elevator at work.

Don't be harsh on yourself. Slow progress is better than no progress. Be proud of yourself for even trying. Remind yourself of how great you are doing because you have earnt it. You are honouring the temple that is your body and that should be recognised.

Beautify Rooms

The feminine woman also likes to beautify her home. Your home, or your bedroom, is the place where you recharge your energetic batteries. The vibe that your room represents is going to have a heavy effect on your feminine energy.

Your place should be an expression of freshness and neatness. When your space is cluttered, it adds a vibe of instability to your energy. Take pride in being clean and organised. The tidier you are, the calmer you'll be and the less anxious you'll feel.

You have the power to design your space in a way that represents beauty. Decorate, style and nurture your environment. Consider bringing nature into your home. Bring plants into your living room or get flowers to beautify your kitchen side.

SISTERHOOD

Be around femininity

One of the most empowering things that you could do to recharge your femininity is to be around other feminine women. It helps you embody femininity, as other women reinforce the principles, thoughts and behaviours that are expressed from feminine energy.

Humans learn best from osmosis. And we certainly become like the people we hang around with the most. Energy multiplies the more that it is in the presence of energy that's of the same frequency. So, when you are around positive, powerful feminine energy, it naturally supercharges your feminine vibe.

If femininity is what you desire, then being in a social circle that is filled with healthy, empowered feminine women should be one of your top priorities. This is no understatement.

We are social pack animals and the tribe we align with is extremely influential.

It's not just about being around other women. It is about aligning with women who you would be genuinely proud to call 'sister'. Women are designed for community. Femininity is all about supportiveness, openness, connection and assistance. Women are naturally skilled at communication, with a great capacity to create and flourish with togetherness.

In ancient times, women understood the power of healthy sisterhood. This was the case in cultures that were heavily aligned with nature. But in a society that seeks to dissolve natural principles and the distinct differences between the sexes, the value of sisterhood has been lost.

Even more worryingly, the mass media instigates feminine competition. For example, it is common to see women fighting on television for the sake of our entertainment. This is deeply saddening and it is no shock that women today do not value sisterhood.

For the sake of temporary entertainment, people are okay with watching a talk show that shows two women pulling each other's hair out over a man who has cheated on them. Or take the reality TV shows that depict women being manipulative and passive-aggressive towards each other over a childish disagreement. And what about the internet blogs that thrive on reporting the drama between female celebrities?

Interestingly, it is mostly women who consume content that promotes feminine competition and the pain of other women. The media corporations that are behind this content do not care. They would never take a second to think about the values that are being promoted. Their loyalty is to the millions of dollars that they generate.

But you must stop and think: what effect does this imagery have on your perception of sisterhood? When you consume content like this in front of young girls, who are sensitive to osmosis and mimicking role models, what message does this send? Does it promote the idea of sisterhood or does it help to create distrust for other women? All these things set your perception of other women.

We live in a society that promotes the idea of "women empowerment," but the principles of this campaign do not extend to healthy sisterhood. The campaign that claims to be for women does not promote healthy feminine role models for us to admire. This is why we see more "cat-fighting" than feminine collaboration in the mainstream.

It's crucial to take matters into your own hands and connect with other women that are also on their feminine journey. You can be the example that you needed to see growing up. And the benefits of doing it will be vast.

Many women solely desire masculine men to inspire their femininity. But masculine men are not able to do many things that feminine women can do to nurture their feminine energy.

Benefits

If you would like to engage in healthy sisterhood, then it should not be built on anything superficial. Of course, it's nice to admire the beauty of other women and respect them for it. This is natural. But the beauty of the outside does not automatically translate into the beauty of character.

Sisterhood should be based on the spiritual content of your teammates. Seek to admire them for the feminine frequency that they project and the quality of their personality. This sets the perfect foundation for a sisterhood that reminds you of feminine magnificence and elegance.

Simply being around people that inspire you to be a better woman is a life hack. And since feminine energy is healing energy, the experience that you'll have being in sisterhood with feminine beings will be a curative one.

For anyone that needs emotional care, the emotional support of healthy feminine women is perhaps the most healing experience of all. Women are more in touch with their emotions than men, so this makes sense.

Part of the reason women are great at healing people mentally is because of their capacity to hold space and verbally receive your expression. It's easy to be vulnerable about the things you are going through when you know that you have someone that will simply empathise with you. And if it's needed, feminine women will help walk you through difficult situations in a way that makes you feel cared for.

The sisterhood you have should be a space filled with positivity that heals all the negative expressions that you share with them. This comes from the extremely supportive nature of women. The masculine energy produces hierarchy and competition. But femininity favours equality, encouragement and cooperation.

Women are not shy to give compliments. Giving yourself positive affirmations is always necessary. But it helps to hear it from others too, especially if that is the catalyst that encourages your positive self-talk. So good female friends will help boost your levels of oxytocin and serotonin.

Toxic Traits

Many women do not learn how to engage in healthy sisterhood dynamics. The reality is that many people will bring toxic traits into their friendships that only serve the purpose of maintaining the wounds that you are working on.

There is not an abundance of celebrities and popular role models that represent femininity well. And because society promotes feminine distrust, the bonds of friendship are often built on shaky grounds. You must identify any toxic traits, both in yourself and from others, which will poison the health of your friendships.

It's necessary to acknowledge that almost all women have had bad experiences with female friends. This could have been in the form of gossip, cattiness or betrayal. And these situations could have sowed a slight resentment for femininity.

You may have experienced one of your closest friends trying to steal your partner or even isolating you from the whole friendship group. It could have been a friend competing with you because she was jealous and she may have tried to ruin your reputation with others. Or maybe you've had your sister trying to manipulate you, or a cousin trying to shame you.

These experiences mentally scar women and contribute to a culture that lacks sacred sisterhood. But do not let them taint your perception of other women. One bad apple does not mean the entire tree cannot be trusted. They do not represent femininity as a whole.

If it's possible, try to empathise with women like this. They are women who have not yet healed their wounds. They are suffering from issues that they haven't sorted out. Unhealed women hurt other women because they have not learned how to channel their feminine energy properly.

Realising this helps you to lower your guard. It is natural to fear being judged, hurt and competed with. If a previous friend broke your trust by spilling your secrets, then it is expected that you'll fear your reputation being tarnished.

Simply keep in mind that these things only happen with women who do not operate on a healthy frequency. Don't let this stop you from complimenting other women and creating connections with new women in your life.

Because of the bad experiences, some women may begin to value friendships with men more than with women. But healthy feminine friendships provide value that men cannot. The key is to raise the standard of what it takes to accept someone as a true friend.

Start viewing the women in your circle as the reflection in your mirror. The healthier you are, the better-quality friendships you will attract.

Sit and reflect on the shadow aspects of yourself which may have attracted the bad friends that you had. And accept how you may have been a bad friend in the past. This takes a respectable amount of accountability. But when you do this, it helps to reveal areas that you need to work on.

Forgive those in the past that have abused the value of your friendship. Forgiveness prevents you from operating on the same frequency that attracted them in the first place. Alternatively, if you've been the friend that has treated another woman badly, forgive yourself and accept that that was a different version of you.

Red Flags

When other women interact with you in a toxic way, do not be dragged into behaving in the same way. You are a healthy empowered woman so do not match the low vibration that they're on. Instead, set boundaries or remove them from your life.

If you're having issues with a friend, consider having a heart-to-heart with them to show them the wounds that they need to heal. Before any healing can be done though, it's useful to know the common issues that threaten to ruin healthy feminine friendships.

You should look out for the following behaviours both from yourself and other women:

1. **Judgement:** Unfortunately, many women have a judgemental attitude. They look at other women and find faults to criticise. Having this mindset requires a negative vibe and it shows that you do not view the world through a positive lens.

   If you did, you would find things to admire in other people and you would encourage them to project these qualities. Judgement destroys the confidence of other women and is certainly not in line with the nurturing characteristics of feminine energy.

2. **Jealousy:** Women do not always have to have faults to receive judgement.

Many times, her great qualities are enough to evoke jealousy. This is unfortunate because jealousy puts you in the mentality of scarcity. Jealousy places all your focus on what you do *not* have. It destroys your feminine radiance.

Empowered women are not jealous of other women. If they admire something that another woman has, they are inspired to attain it to the best of their abilities. Stop and ask yourself: do you truly even want what the other person has, or do you see how what they have makes them *feel* and their happiness is what you are truly envious of? Jealousy shines the light on the wounds that you need to heal and the goals which you need to start working towards.

3. **Comparison:** Never get caught up in comparing yourself to other women.

Focus on *your* style. It's natural to look at others, but you should always focus on what you can be inspired by, rather than what you are bitter about.

You should only compare yourself to the person you were yesterday and no more than that. Comparing yourself to others extinguishes your feminine flames. It places you in your head where all your worries live and where you are most likely to question yourself.

When you are watching others, you take the focus away from yourself. Train yourself to love your personality, body and life without the need to constantly compare yourself to others.

Comparing makes you forget all the things that make you powerful. Everyone has things about them that make them special. This goes for *everyone*. If you do not think that this applies to you, then it's a sign that you've done too much comparing.

4. **Competition:** Many women derive a sense of pleasure from feeling superior to their female counterparts. However, the feminine energy is not combative. It is collaborative.

Do not see the success of other women and think that it equals your loss. When one rises, we all rise, and this is especially the case in sisterhood circles. Putting another woman down does not bring you up.

Think of success like one giant flame on a massive candle. Imagine you are holding a candle that represents your life success and the other women around you are holding their candles.

Let's say that one goes up to the giant flame and uses it to light her candle. Her candle being lit does not mean that your candle won't be lit. On the contrary, she can come to you and use the flame from her candle to light yours. This doesn't put out the fire in her candle when she does this. That is what success is like. Another woman's success can be the catalyst of her fulfilment.

EXERCISE: STOP COMPARISONS

When you notice that you are comparing yourself to others, either verbally or mentally, immediately shut this negative talk down. Investigate the reasons that are making you engage in this sort of frequency. Give that part of yourself all the love it needs so that you don't feel the need to compare.

Creating Social Circles

Use your emotional intelligence and intuitive communication to improve the quality of the friendships that you have. If your current friends do not support the woman that you are trying to become, then you have no choice but to distance yourself.

Stay away from people who do not plan to add value to your femininity journey. Girls who bring other women down and struggle to maintain friendships should be avoided. But it is also good to mend the issues of the current relationships you have.

If you do not have a thriving community of women to connect with, it's fine. You don't need many friends, especially at the beginning of your journey. One positive friend is better than having fifteen who are not supportive.

Of course, fifteen friends who want the best for you are better than one. So, you will have to put effort into seeding connections and nurturing these friendships. Commit to investing time into your social life. Put energy into this because it will satisfy your natural need for connection.

If you want to create new friendships, then you will have to go out and make it happen. It is not going to magically happen if you stay inside the house like a hermit crab. How else do you expect these connections to happen? Go to places, gatherings and events where you can meet your future best friends.

Good places to meet healthy feminine beings:

- Local meetups and workshops
- Retreats
- Wellness groups
- Spiritual sharing circles
- Yoga studios
- Meditation classes
- Crystal stores
- Places of religious worship (church, mosque or temple)
- Self-development events
- Creative classes

When you put yourself in the right environment, it is more likely that you will meet women that are on a similar path to you. It will become natural for you to make friends with the right people. You just have to be willing to put yourself out there.

Nurture these friendships. Make time to go out on dinner dates, brunches and movie nights with your girls. It's a time to let go of your worries and have fun. It's your chance to vent about what you're going through and it's an opportunity to network with people who inspire your fire.

EXERCISE: USE SOCIAL MEDIA

One of the best tools at your disposal is social media. It is not just a place to post content, it also widens the net of your communication. Use it well. It is all you need to make new connections with other women who are like you.

Do not be afraid to create connections virtually. Eventually, once familiarity has been established, reach out to them and offer a time to hang out. They will most likely be excited to make new friends with people on the same wavelength as them and you will be thankful that you made the effort.

The Culture of Your Circle

The true significance of sisterhood is in the value that it provides everyone who is a part of it. To get the best out of it, take the time to recognise what you need from your sisters. But it's equally essential to know the value that you bring to the circle too. This adds a sense of purpose to the group.

Sacred sisterhood is not just a bunch of women getting together and having fun. Rather, it is a circle that is founded on certain principles. There must be a respectable culture within your friendships, meaning that there are specific standards that are promoted and behaviours that are discouraged. If everyone sticks to these principles, it will always be a space that promotes you and your sisters to be the best version of themselves.

Acknowledge achievements: When a sister is doing well, be sure to acknowledge her achievements. Be vocal about how proud you are to see her achieving her goals.

Encouragement: Be a source of positive affirmations that encourage your sisters to be their best selves. When you ignite the flames of a sister, you do the same thing for yourself. Be supportive of the women in your circle. Applaud their intuition, their magic and their greatness.

Hold space: Women are amazing listeners. The feminine energy is about receiving. Give your sister the blessing of emotional support when she's in distress. Do not make the topic about you if it's not needed. Provide her with attentive assistance that makes her thankful to have someone like you in her life.

Authenticity: Cheer on the authentic expression of your sisters. Even if you disagree with her viewpoint, inspire her to be her best self. If a sister truly values you, she wants to see you thrive in your truth. So give your sister support that is based on what *they* want, not what *you* want.

High standards: A part of encouraging your sisters to do their best includes helping them when they are slipping into toxic expressions of femininity. It can also mean highlighting when they are not living up to high standards.

In a non-judgemental way, remind them of their power. When you see them engaging in negative self-talk, refresh their memory of how great they are. If you know that they have been lacking discipline lately, lovingly keep them on track.

Accountability: At some point, you're going to have to tell your sisters some truths that they do not want to hear. But this is what reveals who has our highest interests at heart. If you truly want the best for them, then you will need to warn them when they are being self-destructive. They may not want to hear it but it's for their own good.

You will have to distinguish between people who are being negative and those who are simply giving you tough love. Negative people will reveal their toxicity by communicating with you in a disrespectful tone. People who are giving you tough love will not shame you when they are offering their perspective.

Note: Keep in mind that everyone in the sisterhood is supposed to be reciprocating the same energy. So all of these virtues should be returned to you. If not, it is an unfair exchange of value.

CONCLUSION

You have an important part to play in our Earthly experience. The more you nurture yourself, the more the world is nurtured. So never forget that your life has meaning. Your skills, abilities and gifts serve a purpose that benefit everyone that's around you.

Nurturing feminine energy is about sowing the seeds of growth and spurring on the blooming of your best self. You are a spectacular person. The more work that you do on yourself, the deeper you go. I can promise you that the deeper you go, the more you connect with that spectacular woman who already lies beneath the surface.

You deserve the best that life has to offer. You deserve great experiences. You deserve to look in the mirror and say "wow, I'm so glad to see this reflection." You are becoming your dream person and the pleasure that awaits will be worth all the work.

The path of elevation is not always simple. So I implore you to stay committed and never stop feeding the flowers of your femininity. Protecting the flourishing of this plant may require you to shield it from people you previously thought could be trusted. This could be friends or even family members.

If there's a choice between progressing towards your higher self or gaining the acceptance of others, *always* choose yourself. You are the priority in your life and you should never feel shame for this. You come first! Anyone that does not support your growth does not need to be in your life.

Do not remain attached to the things that do not nurture your power. Let it go if it does not serve you. It may feel unfamiliar and testing but that's exactly what makes it worth it. The future version of yourself yearns for you to stay committed. She depends on you to do work. Don't let her down.

When you make this declaration to yourself, it will keep you on the right path and ensure that you do whatever needs to be done.

So with an abundance of belief in what you are capable of, I wish you all the luck in the world on your journey to nurturing your feminine powers.

ENDING PAGE

This information is only a small step into the journey of feminine development – so you can nurture your femininity. These are designed to be easy-to-digest books that cover only a few topics. There is much more to femininity that was not covered in this book, such as embracing softness, expressing femininity whilst at work or how to attract a healthy masculine man. But this is a gradual journey, and not a quick race, so I intentionally left more to be discovered in the future volumes of this 'Femininity Series'.

I hope to see you in the next volume but until then I'll say this: *nurture yourself and share that power with the world*. Before anyone else, you come first. Never feel bad about this.

The more you nurture yourself, the better you'll be. And the more quality that you have, the more beneficial it is for anyone around you.

If there are any specific topics you would like me to include in the future volumes, then you can email me at: ReemusBailey@GMAIL.com or comment/message on one of my social media accounts: @ReemusB (TikTok & Instagram).